We join **FREE** and **Dr. Michael Maling**
in celebrating the completion of the
Michael S. Maling Torah Scroll

*"Just as my ancestors planted
trees for my sake, so too I plant
for those who will follow me."*
– Talmud Tractate Ta'anit, 23a

By Mendel Kalmenson, culled from the *My Encounter with the Rebbe* project

Cover Art by Annita Soble

Cover and book design by Hannabi Creative

Printed in the United States of America by The Printhouse

Fourth Impression, May 2014

ISBN 9781932349009

Dedicated to the Rebbe,
whose seeds of wisdom continue
to be nurtured in the lives of so many.

Joyfully sponsored in part by
Dr. Michael S. Maling
and the Crain-Maling Foundation

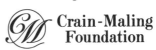
Crain-Maling
Foundation

This project was generously funded in part by
Uri and Bassie Laber

SEEDS OF WISDOM

Culled from *My Encounter with the Rebbe* interviews

JEWISH EDUCATIONAL MEDIA

· SECTION I ·

NURTURING THE HUMAN SPIRIT

· SECTION 2 ·

PARENTING

· SECTION 3 ·

KNOWLEDGE AND LEARNING

· SECTION 4 ·

LOVE AND RELATIONSHIPS

· SECTION 5 ·

FAITH AND PRAYER

· SECTION 6 ·

JEWISH LEADERSHIP

· SECTION 6 ·

JEWISH LEADERSHIP *(continued)*

· PREFACE ·

This book is not about the Rebbe's piety. Nor is it about his character or his scholarship.

It's not about his sensitivity, his leadership, nor his contribution to the Jewish people. In fact, one might say that this book is not really about the Rebbe at all.

It doesn't tell the story of his life. Rather, it aims to enhance yours.

The heartwarming interactions of the Rebbe recounted in this book and the life lessons that can be gleaned from them, were composed in the hope that they might add clarity and meaning to your life's journey.

This is a small book of big ideas, hence the title: *Seeds of Wisdom.*

As a finite seed contains infinite potential, the stories in this book, while small in size, are great in import. As a seed in the palm of one's hand cannot take root until planted firmly in the ground, where it begins to reach its life-giving potential, these seeds of wisdom similarly contain no value until they are contemplated and internalized, unpacked and applied. Only then do these bursts of insight lead to personal growth and meaningful change.

If you discover yourself in the following pages, and if your life is enriched and deepened by absorbing their content, then this book will have achieved its goal.

It is my prayer that these *Seeds of Wisdom* make a difference in my readers' lives.

But just as a seed must be nurtured and cultivated in order to bear fruit, the impact these stories have depends solely on you, their gardener.

—MENDEL KALMENSON
London, 2013

· A NOTE ·

I'd like to make an important observation about the stories in this book.

If there's one rule I've learned from researching the Rebbe's responses to people and situations, it is that there are no rules. More than he answered questions, the Rebbe had a knack for answering people. His genius lay not in bundling people and situations together, but in discerning and appreciating the subtleties of each dilemma—seeing how each person and every situation was unique.

The stories are therefore presented as relevant and thought-provoking personal encounters with the Rebbe, not universal advice to be applied in every similar situation.

Also, the often whimsical one-line takeaways at the end of each story are no more than my own interpretations.

They're intended as points of departure to help you apply the meaning of the story, rather than as final destinations. Not everyone will glean the same lessons from every story.

I've tried to stick with "universal truisms," but ultimately each person and every situation is unique.

M.K.

· THE REBBE ·

The Lubavitcher Rebbe, Rabbi Menachem Mendel Schneerson (1902-1994), of righteous memory, was the seventh leader in the Chabad-Lubavitch dynasty.

He is considered one the most influential religious personalities of modern times. People of all faiths, nationalities and backgrounds sought his advice and counsel, traveling from across the world to receive his blessing and guidance.

More than any other individual, the Rebbe was responsible for stirring the conscience of world Jewry, leading to a spiritual awakening that continues to be felt today.

To his hundreds of thousands of followers and millions of admirers around the world, he was—and remains today, following his passing—"the Rebbe."

NURTURING THE
HUMAN SPIRIT

THE CANDLE

Late one night, two hours into an audience with the
Rebbe, the Israeli diplomat Yehuda Avner asked, "Rebbe,
what is it that you seek to accomplish?"

"Yehuda," said the Rebbe to Avner, "look there, on the
shelf. What is that you see?"

"A candle," he replied.

"No, it's not a candle; it's just a lump of wax with a string
down the middle. When does this lump of wax become a
candle? When you bring a flame to the wick."

His voice rising, the Rebbe continued in a Talmudic sing-
song: "The wax is the body of the human being, and the
wick is the soul. The flame is the fire of Torah. When
the soul is ignited by the flame of Torah, that's when the
person becomes a candle, achieving the purpose for which
he was created.

"This is what I try to do—to help every man and woman achieve the purpose for which they were created."

An hour later, with the sun about to rise and the meeting drawing to a close, Avner asked, "So has the Rebbe lit my candle?"

"No," answered the Rebbe quietly. "I have given you the match. Only you can light your own candle."

*To help someone
is to put them on their feet,
not on your shoulders.*

HUNGRY PRAYERS

"Tell me something," the Rebbe once asked an individual during a conversation pertaining to faith, "do you pray each morning?"

"I do," the man responded, "but very hurriedly."

"Why is that?" the Rebbe asked.

"Because when I wake up in the morning I am very weak due to my bad nerves," said the man. "I was taught that Jewish law forbids eating before praying, so when I pray first thing in the morning, I am not at my best."

"The way I see it," the Rebbe said kindly, "you must eat something first thing in the morning. Due to your condition, you can even have a full meal, if need be.

"The Tzemach Tzedek once told someone in a similar situation, 'It's better to eat in order to pray, than to pray in order to eat.'"[1]

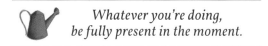 *Whatever you're doing,*
be fully present in the moment.

HEALTHY DISSATISFACTION

Yitzhak Rabin, the late Prime Minister of Israel, was at a *yechidut* with the Rebbe. "How are you?" the Rebbe asked him warmly. "I can't complain," Prime Minister Rabin responded, "life is good."

The Rebbe replied, "It's true that our sages teach: 'Who is rich? One who is satisfied with what he has,' but this applies only to material wealth.

"When it comes to spiritual matters, however, one must never be content with one's current state. No matter how much one has achieved, he must strive for more tomorrow."

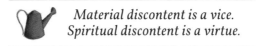

Material discontent is a vice.
Spiritual discontent is a virtue.

A SURVIVOR'S PREDICAMENT

A survivor of the Holocaust came to see the Rebbe. "I can't stop living in the past," he confided. "A dark shadow constantly hangs over my life, and I can't help but view life through the prism of my traumatized past."

"Have you ever spoken about your experiences?" the Rebbe asked gently.

"No, I haven't," the gentleman responded. "I find it too painful."

"Then I suggest you write a memoir," the Rebbe advised, "and make sure to write it yourself, not through a ghost writer."

In order to turn a new page,
you might need to complete
the previous chapter.

TUNNEL VISION

An individual who had decided to change careers visited the Rebbe, seeking guidance and blessing.

Advising him on how to adjust to his new environment, the Rebbe suggested; "For the first three to six months don't ask yourself where this is going, because you won't have the answer. You can't always judge your success in the moment."

 *Constant evaluation
can stifle growth.*

GROWING UP

Lacking the confidence to attend his audience with the Rebbe by himself, a 14-year-old *yeshiva* student arrived with his father in tow.

"Why did you bring your father along?" the Rebbe asked gently.

"It is time," he added sympathetically, "that you become your own *mensch*. You have the power to stand on your own."

Thereafter, whenever the young man's father would ask a question on behalf of his son, the Rebbe would respond:

"Let your son come and ask for himself; he must learn to become his own person."

 You cannot leap
if someone else is carrying you.

THE KEYS TO CHANGE

A young man who was struggling with bad habits requested the Rebbe's advice. He had tried to improve his behavior, but found that his resolve was too often defeated by his deep-seated impulses.

"How can I achieve a lasting transformation?" he asked.

The Rebbe responded: "The *key* to real change is to firmly resolve in your heart of hearts that this behavior doesn't reflect who you truly are.

"But the *first step* toward freeing yourself of the habit is to avoid the situations that trigger it in the first place."

 "It's not the mouse who steals. It's the hole it climbs through that's responsible for the theft." —TALMUD[2]

A POWERFUL TITLE

Philanthropists Count and Countess Maklouf Elkaim,
were reluctant to use their inherited titles, deeming it
pretentious to do so.

The Rebbe addressed their hesitation at a private
audience: "Since, by Divine Providence, you possess these
prestigious titles, don't hesitate to use them to open doors
for Jewish causes. People will take you more seriously if you
introduce yourselves as 'Count and Countess.' Others may
use their titles egotistically, but as Jews, you should use this
unique privilege to impact the people you meet."

If used properly,
vanity can produce virtue.

NOBEL PASSION

A graduate student once visited the Rebbe to discuss his academic career. During their conversation, the Rebbe shared an anecdote:

"While studying at the University of Berlin, I attended an introductory course by a professor who had won a Nobel Prize years earlier. Initially, I couldn't understand why such an accomplished professor would be teaching an introductory course!"

The Rebbe continued with a smile. "But then I learned that teachers at the university were paid according to the number of students they taught. Since there were many more students taking the introductory course than the advanced course, he chose to teach the less challenging course, because it provided a better salary!"

Be true to yourself and your passions at all costs.

HOW TO CHANGE PATHS

A successful teacher sought the Rebbe's advice regarding his next career move. The school where he'd taught for 13 years was opening a second branch in another city, and he'd been offered the principal's job.

"While I'm comfortably settled in my current job, taking on a more challenging role might be good for me," the teacher said. He paused, and then ventured:

"Besides, if the new school fails, my current school has promised to hold a teaching position for me, so I'll always have that to fall back on."

The Rebbe's response was candid. "If this new position is attractive because your old job remains available in the event of failure, then you should stay in your old job," he counseled. "Only commit to the new job if you truly believe that failure is not an option. That mindset will help ensure that you make your new job succeed."

 In order to advance forward, you might need to burn the bridges leading you back.

A COSTLY COMPLIMENT

A *chasid* would constantly update the Rebbe with news of his communal activities. He asked whether the Rebbe was happy with the work he had reported.

The Rebbe smiled and replied: "Happy, I most certainly am—but by nature, I'm never satisfied with what has already been done, in an area where even more can be achieved."

The Rebbe continued softly, "Somehow, I feel this is a part of my nature that I needn't change."

 "One who has one hundred desires two hundred." —MIDRASH[3]

DETERMINING YOUR DESTINY

When Sir Jonathan Sacks, the Chief Rabbi of Great Britain, first visited the Rebbe as a college student, the Rebbe asked him: "What are you doing for Jewish life at Cambridge University?"

"Well," Rabbi Sacks began to explain, "in the situation in which I find myself…"

The Rebbe interrupted: "No one ever '*finds* himself in a situation.' People *put* themselves in situations. And if you put yourself in one situation, you can put yourself in a different one."

 We are co-authors in our destiny.

A DOSE OF ALTRUISM

A sought-after lecturer on Jewish topics was once
speaking with the Rebbe. At the end of their exchange, the
Rebbe advised him gently:

"Perhaps it would be a good idea for you to give a class
at least once a week free of charge, in accordance with the
teaching of our sages, 'One should serve G-d not for the sake
of reward.'"

*Serving G-d selflessly
is the greatest reward of all.*

BROTHERHOOD

Since his youth, Hershel had a privileged relationship with the Rebbe. He was a brilliant scholar who often consulted the Rebbe on questions he encountered in his Talmudic studies. After the Rebbe assumed the mantle of Chabad leadership, Hershel called on the Rebbe to wish him success in his holy undertaking. He felt close enough to ask: "*Nu*? So how do you like being Rebbe?"

The Rebbe responded: "What I miss most are the informal *farbrengens* of old. These days, I speak and the *chasidim* listen. But there's nothing like sitting among the *chasidim* and *farbrenging* together in unity."

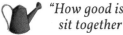

"How good is it is when brothers sit together as one!" —PSALMS[4]

LABOR OF LOVE

A British school teacher visited the Rebbe for a private audience. As per the protocol at *yechidut*, he handed the Rebbe his note, outlining some of his innovations and accomplishments in the classroom over the past year.

After reading the note, the Rebbe looked up and studied the man, a serious expression on his face. "You seem disappointed, Rebbe," the teacher said. "Have I done something wrong? Is something the matter with my teaching?"

The Rebbe responded gently: "While it is obvious from your report that you are devoted to your mission, I do not perceive that you find joy in your work."

It's not enough to be good at it,
the key to success
is loving what you do.

THE BIRTHDAY CHALLENGE

In a discussion on education, the Rebbe told a rabbi:
"Jewish education must communicate that Judaism is not a
religion of ceremony but of celebration and experience. Jews
must be taught that their tradition not only commemorates
a rich and ancient past. Their religion is alive, linking the
past to the present in a real and relevant way."

Later in the conversation, the rabbi mentioned to the
Rebbe that he was celebrating his birthday. The Rebbe
smiled and said: "A birthday poses the very same challenge.
On one's birthday, he can either commemorate an event
that happened years ago, or he can experience it as though
it had just occurred, as if he was just given a new life and a
new purpose."

Birth is G-d's way of saying,
"You matter."
Birthdays are His reminder.

ON GIVING

A philanthropist who had recently funded the building of a Jewish school came to see the Rebbe. The Rebbe congratulated him on his good work. As they continued with their conversation, the Rebbe took issue with the practice of allocating charity to "fashionable" causes.

"The common English translation of the Hebrew word *tzedaka* is 'charity,' which connotes magnanimity, positioning the giver in the seat of power," the Rebbe declared. "In reality, this translation is a mistake; it couldn't be further from the true meaning of *tzedaka*!"

"The root of the word *tzedaka* is '*tzedek*,' which means 'justice,'" the Rebbe explained. "When G-d blesses one with wealth, it's His way of saying, 'I trust you to distribute some of these funds responsibly.'

"In Jewish tradition, giving to those who have less is an obligation. To give of one's money is not just a nice thing to do, it's the *right* thing—the *just* thing."

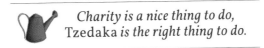

Charity is a nice thing to do,
Tzedaka *is the right thing to do.*

GRAND PLANS

A senior *chasid* who had been devoted to the previous Lubavitcher Rebbe came to see the Rebbe on a personal matter.

"Rebbe, I recently had a dream in which your father-in-law challenged me to become involved in a certain charitable cause," he said. "I responded that I was already involved in a similar one, to which the previous Rebbe replied, 'If that's the case, get involved on a small scale.'"

A bit sheepishly the *chasid* continued, "Normally, I would not have taken up your time with mere dreams, but our sages teach that if a person has a very clear dream they should take it to heart, and my dream was incredibly clear. What should I make of this?"

The Rebbe was very serious as he listened to the elder *chasid*. "In my opinion," he responded, "it's a significant dream, and you should fulfill it." Smiling, he continued:

"But our sages teach that 'there is no dream without pointless words.'[5] I believe that the pointless words in your dream are, 'on a small scale.' Get involved in a big way!"

 When it comes to a good deed, don't be too calculating.

ON DECISION-MAKING

The father of a young man visited the Rebbe to share his frustration: "If only the Rebbe would help my son decide whom to marry, I'm sure he would be married in no time!"

"I don't like to make *shidduch* decisions for my *chasidim*," the Rebbe responded. "If he would make this major determination based on my choice, he might later regret a decision that wasn't truly his own. Perhaps he'd be married quickly, but would he be married *happily*?"

*The larger the decision,
the greater the need for volition.*

THE CHALLENGING TASK

Rabbi Zev Segal, a well-respected Jewish activist, shared a close relationship with the Rebbe.

Once, before Segal traveled abroad, the Rebbe asked him to undertake a confidential and very challenging assignment.

Upon returning to the United States, Segal reported back to the Rebbe. "Rebbe," he said, "let me tell you; it was not an easy task at all!"

"Rabbi Segal," the Rebbe responded with a smile, "since when did you make a contract with the Al-mighty that your life would be easy?"

 "Man was born to toil." —JOB[6]

LIVING TO THE FULLEST

On the occasion of her birthday, a woman wrote a letter to the Rebbe, mentioning some of her efforts over the past year to share the beauty of Judaism with uninitiated Jews.

After warmly noting her achievements, the Rebbe wrote, "...bear in mind, however, that a person who was granted the ability to impact 100 people and reaches only 99, has not yet fully realized their G-d-given potential."

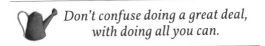

Don't confuse doing a great deal,
with doing all you can.

THE GREATEST GIFT

A *yeshiva* student in "770" started an interest-free loan fund for his fellow students. He posted a sign on the bulletin board with the rules of the fund.

A short while later he was summoned to see the Rebbe. He entered the Rebbe's room nervously, wondering if perhaps he was about to be tested on his studies.

"I saw your sign on the wall stating that you have opened a *gemach*," the Rebbe said.

"Yes, I did, but I'm sorry," the young student said respectfully, "we only make loans to *yeshiva* students."

The Rebbe smiled broadly and said, "I didn't ask to see you for a loan. I'd like to contribute to your wonderful initiative."

After handing the student a check for the *gemach*, the Rebbe said: "I want you to know that the *mitzvah* of lending money is so great that *chasidim* of old used to lend each other money even when it wasn't needed, just in order to fulfill this great *mitzvah*!"

> *"There are eight levels of charity. The highest level, surpassing all the others, is giving a loan to someone, thus supporting him before he falls and becomes needy."*
> —MAIMONIDES[7]

TIRED BUT TRIED

A prominent rabbi visited the Rebbe. He was overwhelmed.
Juggling all of his commitments had become too difficult to
handle, and he needed to cut back on some of them.

"Rebbe," he said wearily, "*ich bin meed*—I am tired."

The Rebbe responded, "I, too, am tired. *Iz vos*—so what?
You must continue the holy work of 'making souls,' which
was begun by our ancestors Abraham and Sarah."

 So what if you're tired?

· SECTION 2 ·

PARENTING

DISCIPLINED APPROACH

"I have a problem," a father confided in the Rebbe. "I lose my temper and to my eternal regret, I even hit my children at times. What can I do to stop this terrible behavior?"

"Contemplate this fact," the Rebbe responded. "As much as they are your children, they are G-d's children too. You wouldn't hit someone else's child, and surely not a child of G-d!

"If you keep this in mind, your hand will tremble before striking your child," the Rebbe concluded gently.

"There are three partners in the creation of a child: the Holy One, the father and mother." —TALMUD[8]

DANCE OF THE TEACHERS

A schoolteacher informed the Rebbe that he was fed up with teaching and was looking for a new career. "There's just not enough appreciation given to teachers," he complained.

The Rebbe responded: "There are those who feel that teaching little children is an undignified position. I, on the other hand, consider 'teacher' to be the highest title of honor."

"You know, Maimonides writes that in the Holy Temple, only Israel's greatest—the *rashei yeshivot,* members of the high court, and the elders—would dance and rejoice in the Temple on the festival of *Sukkot.* The others, both men and the women, would behold the celebration."[9]

"As a teacher, you are the modern day *rosh yeshiva* that Maimonides is referring to."

Upon hearing the Rebbe express the deep esteem he had for teachers, the man decided to continue teaching.

Encourage the person who takes your child's hand, opens his mind, and touches his heart.

VISUAL EFFECTS

A man came to the Rebbe together with his 10-year-old son. The boy had recently begun studying Talmud, the vast body of rabbinic literature which forms the basis of Jewish Law.

"What topic are you currently studying?" the Rebbe asked the boy.

"We're learning about *shor shenagach et hapara*," the boy replied, referring to the well-known Talmudic passage which discusses the financial obligations of the owner of an ox that gored another's cow.

The Rebbe asked the child, "Have you ever seen an ox or a cow?" The boy replied that he had.

"Where did you see them?" the Rebbe asked.

"In an exhibit on Noah's Ark," he responded.

"Very good," the Rebbe said, clearly satisfied. "Then you can visualize what you are learning about."

Children must understand not only their studies, but also what they are studying about.

MOVING ON

A couple, utterly broken after the loss of their teenage daughter, came to the Rebbe to seek advice. While they were financially and socially settled in their community, they found it difficult to heal in an environment that continually reminded them of their loss.

With gentle warmth, the Rebbe shifted their focus.

"Your other children," he asked, "where can you best raise them lovingly?"

The couple, unsure how to respond, listened closely as the Rebbe guided them.

"If moving to a new environment will open your hearts to healing and allow your family to flourish, fear not the challenges the new place will bring. Follow the path that will nourish your other children.... They need to grow up in an environment of love."

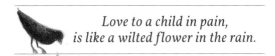

Love to a child in pain,
is like a wilted flower in the rain.

THE HIGHEST DEGREE

A young man decided to explore his Jewish roots and attend a *yeshiva*. His grandparents became very concerned about his future.

"What will become of him?" they asked the Rebbe. "How will he succeed in life if he doesn't have his college degree?"

The Rebbe turned to the woman and asked, "Tell me about *your* grandparents."

Her face lit up. "My grandmother was a very special lady. She would distribute charity with an open hand. Her knowledge of Judaism was so great that she would converse with the rabbinic scholars who would visit her home. She was a very unique woman," the woman concluded, glowing.

The Rebbe then turned to her husband, inquiring about his grandparents. He told the Rebbe that his grandfather had been a well-known *chasid* in Poland, a man he admired deeply. His fondest childhood memories were of the time spent with his grandfather.

When he finished, the Rebbe asked the couple with a smile, "Would it be so terrible if your grandson turned out like your grandparents?"

Don't confuse what you want your children to have with who you want them to be.

DISCIPLINE

A woman once came to the Rebbe seeking parenting advice.

"Rebbe," she said sadly, "I don't know how to handle my children! I am so torn about disciplining them. I feel so terrible when I punish them!"

The Rebbe responded kindly: "Think of it this way: As difficult as it is, the act of disciplining your child now prevents them from twice as much pain later on."

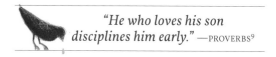

"He who loves his son disciplines him early." —PROVERBS[9]

EQUAL STANDARDS

The father of a Bar Mitzvah boy was in *yechidut*. He told the Rebbe that because his wife had recently lost her father, they had decided to make a modest celebration for the Bar Mitzvah.

"This is not the first Bar Mitzvah you are celebrating in the family...." the Rebbe began.

"Yes, we have an older son whose Bar Mitzvah we celebrated a few years ago," the father replied.

"What you did for your older son, you must do for the younger one. Any disparity might upset the Bar Mitzvah boy at this important stage in his life."

> *"The brothers hated Joseph because of a colorful coat their father Jacob had given to him. One must not differentiate between his children."* —MIDRASH[10]

THE PARAMOUNT BLESSING

After doing a particularly daunting favor for a person close to the Rebbe, a *chasid* figured that he now had the opportunity to ask the Rebbe for a special blessing.

Facing an insurmountable business challenge which threatened his entire enterprise, he requested a blessing that everything miraculously fall into place.

The Rebbe's penetrating response left a lasting impression on him. "If you have the chance to ask for anything in the world, how could you ask for anything other than *yiddishe nachas* from your children?!"

There's no greater blessing than the gift of nachas *from your children.*

LESSON IN FAITH

Before his Bar Mitzvah, Rabbi Mordechai Einbinder joined his father for a private audience with the Rebbe. When they were about to leave, the Rebbe turned to the young boy and said earnestly, "When you grow up I would like you to be my *shliach*."

Many years later, Rabbi Einbinder reminisced: "That one sentence the Rebbe uttered to me as a Bar Mitzvah boy had a profound impact on me. In those few words, the Rebbe communicated his confidence in me. They touched me deeply and shaped my life.

"When things become difficult, I always remember the Rebbe's faith in me."

*Believe in a child
and he will believe in himself.*

A MEANINGFUL BAR MITZVAH

A woman and her children came to a private audience with the Rebbe in festive attire. Feeling awkward and overdressed, the woman excused their fancy clothes, explaining that they had just come from the Bar Mitzvah of a relative. The Rebbe asked: "And how did the Bar Mitzvah boy prepare for his auspicious day?"

She replied: "After months of practice, he did a wonderful job reading the entire Torah portion for family and friends!"

After complimenting the boy's hard work, the Rebbe said: "The amount of time and effort some young boys spend preparing for a one-time ceremony could better be devoted to studying the meaning of becoming a responsible Jewish adult!"[11]

A Bar Mitzvah can last a day
or it can last a lifetime.

NO EXCUSES

A number of young children in a particular community died under tragic circumstances. Their parents feared that this was punishment for bad deeds they had committed. They went to the Rebbe seeking a *tikkun*, a spiritual rectification.

"A *tikkun*?" the Rebbe replied. "You must know that you've done nothing wrong."

The Rebbe continued: "It is the way of our world that when a slap is given, it is given to the face. Not because the face committed a greater wrong, but because it is the purest representation of the whole individual. The ones who take the hit are the purest."

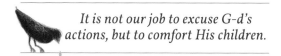

It is not our job to excuse G-d's actions, but to comfort His children.

ROCKET SCIENCE

Professor Velvl Green, a scientist working for NASA, was once discussing space travel with the Rebbe. The Rebbe brought up a problem for which NASA had found an ingenious solution.

In order to move a spaceship from the ground to the space beyond Earth's atmosphere, a great amount of thrust is needed, which is generated by fuel.

The problem is that in order to push a heavy object, a large amount of fuel is required. To hold more fuel, a larger container is essential. A larger container means more weight, which demands more thrust, and thereafter more fuel, and consequently a larger container, and so on....

"NASA solved this problem," the Rebbe said admiringly, "and their solution carries a lesson in serving G-d."

The Rebbe explained: "They created the Saturn Rocket with a number of stages. First, the huge thruster that lifts the rocket from earth overcomes the pull of gravity. It's fed by a huge fuel tank, but once that fuel is used up, the container is dead weight. So the container is discarded, leaving them with a lighter load. Now, a lesser amount of fuel can take them farther, and when the fuel from the second and lighter container is used, this container is discarded, as well. The same is done after each stage, continually lightening the load and enabling farther travel."

"And the lesson for us?" the professor asked.

"The verse states, 'Educate the child according to his own path.'[12] When he's a little child, you reward him with sweets—it's something petty, but it helps propel him forward.

"When he starts learning a little more, you change the incentive—perhaps a bicycle.

"When he's past that particular stage, his motivation for material or spiritual advancement becomes more advanced.

"As he grows and matures, what was previously considered 'fuel' may now become dead weight and can hinder, rather than help advance, his spiritual journey. It must be discarded and traded in for a higher form of motivation and inspiration."

*What propelled
you forward yesterday
might hold you back today.*

AN ENVIABLE POSITION

In 1941, the sixth Lubavitcher Rebbe, Rabbi Yosef
Yitzchak Schneersohn, instituted a program that provided
Jewish children from New York City public schools with an
hour of weekly Jewish study.

Every Wednesday afternoon, student volunteers from
the Lubavitch *yeshiva* interrupt their studies for several
hours, travel to New York City's public schools, bring
their charges to local synagogues, teach them about their
traditions, and then escort them back to their respective
schools.

One studious young man wrote to the Rebbe, asking to
be excused from participating in the program, as he felt he
was wasting his time.

First, he wrote, he didn't think that he actually achieved
very much. Every week he recited prayers with the
children, but didn't believe that the prayer sessions had any
lasting effect.

Second, it took three or four hours out of his day to travel to the school assigned to him, pick up the children, teach them, drop them off, and then return to the *yeshiva*. He felt that his time would be better spent furthering his studies.

The Rebbe replied: "I want you to know that on Wednesday afternoons, all of the souls in *Gan Eden*, including Moses himself, envy you for the unique opportunity you have each week to say *Shema Yisrael* and recite a blessing with a Jewish child. Their souls no longer have the opportunity to interact with Jewish children and bring them closer to their Father in Heaven. Do you know what they would give for the privilege that you have?"

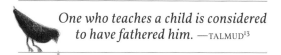

One who teaches a child is considered to have fathered him. —TALMUD[13]

KNOWLEDGE AND LEARNING

GETTING TO THE SOURCE

Ending a meeting with a group of students, the Rebbe smiled and said: "Well, I've asked you lots of questions; would any of you like to ask me a question?"

One fellow spoke up. "As a matter of fact, I would," he said. "I've heard all kinds of stories about you. They say that you know better than the doctor whether to perform a surgery. You know better than the lawyer whether to proceed with the case.

"How can that be? Do you know more about medicine than the doctors or more law than the lawyers?"

The Rebbe smiled. "When a house is being built, the architect draws up a blueprint and gives it to the contractor, who then directs the plumber regarding his trade, and the electrician regarding his trade, and so on. You see, it's not that the contractor can do the work better than the others; he simply knows how to read the blueprint and so he is able to give the instructions."

"The same is true of our world," the Rebbe continued, quoting the *Midrash*: "'G-d, the Master Architect, used the Torah as the blueprint for creation.'[14] The more in touch we are with Torah, the more sensitive we become to the inner workings of creation."

If you want to know how it works, study the manual.

FLIGHT INSTRUCTION

Rabbi Moshe Feller, the senior *shliach* to Minnesota, invited the Pulitzer Prize-winning author Herman Wouk to give the keynote address at Lubavitch of Minnesota's annual dinner.

On their way to the dinner, Rabbi Feller was amazed to hear Wouk say that he'd derived his greatest sense of accomplishment yet from finishing the study of the whole *Mishna,* the first major work of rabbinic Judaism, for the first time.

The dinner was a great success, and at the last moment Rabbi Feller was inspired to join Wouk on his private flight to Washington, D.C. He would then continue onto New York, where he'd report to the Rebbe personally on the success of the dinner.

Rabbi Feller was excited at the thought of using the two-hour flight to interview one of the greatest novelists of the day about his life and interests.

But as he boarded the small plane and sat down across

from Wouk, he thought to himself: "Am I a journalist or a rabbi? Will satisfying my curiosity be the best way to utilize this opportunity?" Feller took out the Passover *Haggada* he had with him, and instead imparted insights on the text which he had learned from the Rebbe. Mr. Wouk shared his own ideas and insights, and they had a remarkable discussion about the upcoming holiday.

After arriving in New York, Rabbi Feller jumped in a cab, reaching "770" at 2:30 A.M. He hurriedly wrote and submitted a brief report about the dinner of the previous evening. Shortly afterwards, the Rebbe summoned Rabbi Feller.

Feller's heart skipped a beat as he entered the Rebbe's study. With a twinkle in his eye, the Rebbe asked, "And what did you talk about on the plane?"

View every opportunity
as a calling.

A GOOD SCHOOL

A young girl's parents allowed her to choose between two Jewish schools they had selected.

One school was academically superior, while the other placed greater emphasis on good character than on good marks.

She decided to consult the Rebbe about her choice.

"First and foremost," the Rebbe responded, "you must look at which school will help you best develop as a human being and as a Jew."

School is where characters develop, not just careers.

A DEFINITION OF MAZAL

A schoolteacher who struggled financially complained to the Rebbe, "Rebbe, it seems as if I have no *mazal*!"

The Rebbe replied, "No *mazal*? You are the luckiest man alive! You have the opportunity to guide children in the ways of Torah, impacting their entire lives!"

There is no greater honor than the responsibility to mold future generations.

IN THE VERNACULAR

The principal of a large *chasidic* school came to see the Rebbe. He was considering changing the language used by teachers in his school from Yiddish to English, but many of the parents were opposed. For generations, their children had been taught in Yiddish, the *mame lashon* spoken by their grandparents, and they didn't want this rich tradition to be lost. In reality, however, most of the children struggled with Yiddish, and this was having a negative effect on their studies.

"Rebbe," the principal said, "I don't want to be the one responsible for discontinuing this longstanding tradition, but the children are struggling to learn in a language they aren't fluent in."

The Rebbe asked pointedly, "What language do the children speak on the playground?"

"English," he responded.

"Then that should be the language of their studies," the Rebbe said.

"Tell the parents who want their children to be taught in Yiddish, that they surely also want their children to grow up to be Torah-observant Jews. If their children will be taught their formal studies in Yiddish, which is foreign to them, they may develop a distaste for everything they learn, which, in turn, will affect their *yiddishkeit*.

"If the parents want the children to learn Yiddish, the teachers can speak to the children in Yiddish during playtime, and when telling them stories."

Don't confuse the essential with the peripheral.

COST-BENEFIT ANALYSIS

A school administrator complained to the Rebbe that, due to the many discounts being given to families in need, his school was constantly in the red.

"It seems that the only way we can balance our budget once and for all is to eliminate all tuition breaks, even if it means losing some of our students. It's not the end of the world; they can always augment their Jewish education when they get a bit older."

The Rebbe responded pointedly: "With all due respect, you've got it wrong. It's money that can always be replenished, not one's youth."

> *"One who learns Torah in his childhood is like ink inscribed on fresh paper."* —ETHICS OF THE FATHERS[15]

PROSPECTING FOR GREATNESS

A young educator who established a friendly rapport with his students was advised to adopt a more distant manner. "The children don't need a friend in you," he was told. "What they need is an authority figure."

On a visit to New York, the young man consulted the Rebbe on the matter. When he mentioned the critique he had received, the Rebbe assumed a serious demeanor.

"Today's children," the Rebbe said, "do not need to be overly criticized or lectured about their shortcomings. They are their own biggest critics. Instead, they need to hear more about their strengths and incredible potential."

A wise teacher knows who a child is, and shows him who he can become.

MITZVOT DEFINED

A young rabbi who had built a Jewish day school came
to the Rebbe. "Rebbe, maybe I am wasting my effort," he
said glumly. "When I opened our day school, I was idealistic
about teaching *yiddishkeit* to Jewish kids and helping them
become better Jews. But no matter how much I teach
them, when they go home, none of it is reinforced or even
encouraged. In fact, the parents always seem to counteract
all of my work! I think I should go into another line of work."

The Rebbe discouraged him from resigning. To illustrate
his point, he shared a legal case with the rabbi: "Let's say
a terrible criminal is sentenced to die. On the way to be
executed, he asks for a glass of water. Even though he is
about to die, he is nonetheless obligated to recite a blessing
of gratitude over the water, and those who hear his blessing
are required to answer 'Amen.'

"Why is this? A blessing or good deed is inherently valuable, irrespective of everything else surrounding it—even the long-term effect on the one who performs it."

"Imagine then the value of the blessings and good deeds of these pure and innocent children!"

Concluded the Rebbe: "You are teaching Torah and performing *mitzvot* with pure Jewish children. Regardless of the outcome, the value of every *mitzvah* you do with them is infinite!"

A mitzvah *is not only a means to an end. It is an end unto itself.*

A MAN OF LETTERS

As a physics student at Pennsylvania State University, Dr. Yaakov Hanoka took a year's break from pursuing his PhD to study Judaism in a *yeshiva*. He became so enamored with Torah-true Judaism that he wanted to remain in the *yeshiva* instead of continuing with his doctorate.

Toward the end of his first year he had an audience with the Rebbe, during which he brought up his plans for the future. Much to his surprise, the Rebbe said, "I want you to go back to the University to get your PhD."

"But Rebbe," Dr. Hanoka countered respectfully, "if I stay on in *yeshiva*, perhaps I can become a campus rabbi and go on to share my experience and religious passion with Jewish students, inspiring them to learn more about their heritage."

The Rebbe answered with a smile:

"You will accomplish more for *yiddishkeit* with three initials after your name."

Some see a PhD as a way to advance in the world; others see a PhD as a way to advance the world.

OPEN-MINDED

A *yeshiva* student visited the Rebbe to discuss his academic progress. During their conversation, the Rebbe encouraged him during his free time to study, those topics that he found most interesting, independent of the *yeshiva* curriculum.

"But, Rebbe," the student asked, "I've heard it said in the name of the *chasidic* masters that one's initial and natural desires usually reflect one's less-refined side. Shouldn't I study what is less enjoyable, and thereby accustom myself to doing that which I don't like to?"

The Rebbe clarified: "When one wishes to develop himself and refine his character, he can invest his energies and resources into taming his desires. But when it comes to our intellectual pursuits, our sages taught, 'One should always study the part of Torah which his heart desires.'"[16]

> *The mind operates at its best*
> *when it is willingly engaged.*

TENDING THE VINEYARD

In 1965, the Rebbe urged Rabbi Nachman Bernhard to bolster Jewish life in South Africa by taking a position in the country's largest synagogue. At the time, there was no proper Jewish schooling in South Africa.

"Rebbe," he said respectfully: "While I appreciate the need to build proper schools for the Jewish community there, what about my own children?"

The Rebbe replied, "G-d will look out for your children. But you must selflessly help the community, as the verse laments, 'They made me a keeper of the vineyards; but my own vineyard I did not keep.'"[17]

"Quite the contrary!" Rabbi Bernhard objected. "The verse supports my approach. You are making me a guardian of others' vineyards, but what about my vineyard—my own children?"

"Your own?" the Rebbe replied. "And what should every Jewish child in South Africa be considered, if not your own?"

"All Jews are responsible for one-another." —TALMUD[18]

A SCHEDULE FOR LIVING

A young man had put his graduate degree on hold to attend *yeshiva*, and was struggling with the transition. He came to see the Rebbe for advice.

"I am having a problem keeping to the structure and schedule of *yeshiva* life," he revealed. In graduate school, he explained, he used to work nights in the lab, and start his days in the early afternoon.

"How necessary, really, is this rigid schedule?" the student asked. "As long as I study the same amount of hours, isn't that good enough?"

"A human being needs boundaries and a framework for living," the Rebbe responded. "A structured life is not only more efficient, it also satisfies the basic human craving for consistency and security.

"Personally," the Rebbe concluded, "I have found having a set schedule to be very helpful in my own life."

Structured living doesn't limit, it liberates.

CREDENTIALS TO TEACH

A *chasid* was stepping into a new educational role
and was suddenly worried that he didn't have enough
knowledge and experience to fill the position. He came to
see the Rebbe, asking whether he had the right to assume
this new role.

The Rebbe asked him encouragingly, "Do you know *Aleph*?"

Not quite sure what the Rebbe meant by his question,
the *chasid* nodded, "Yes." After all, any Jewish preschooler
knows *Aleph*!

"Then teach *Aleph*!" the Rebbe exclaimed with conviction
and warmth.

"If you were blessed with the gift of knowledge, you have
the responsibility to share that knowledge with others."

*You don't have to know everything
in order to teach something.*

MAIMONIDES' TRUE FACE

A scholar came to see the Rebbe about a question that was bothering him. His exploration of Jewish texts had brought him to study Maimonides, the great Jewish teacher and philosopher of the Middle Ages, and the author of several monumental works, including *Mishneh Torah*, a comprehensive compendium of practical Jewish Law, and *Morah Nevuchim, the Guide for the Perplexed*—a work of philosophy.

The man observed, "Each of these works seemingly reflects a very different, and sometimes contradictory, face of this legendary Jewish teacher! But which of his works represents the real Maimonides?" he asked.

The Rebbe responded: "The true Maimonides is seen in his work on Jewish law. It is a practical work with clear instructions for life."

With a hint of a smile the Rebbe advised: "Better study the *Mishneh Torah* and learn how to live as a Jew, than memorize the *Guide to the Perplexed* and know the answer to questions you didn't even have."

"The deed is paramount."
—ETHICS OF THE FATHERS[19]

BRIDGES OF TRADITION

During a meeting with Mr. Joseph Cayre, a business leader in the recording industry, and a prominent member of the Sephardic community, the Rebbe expressed great interest in the spiritual state of the Sephardic community, and asked specifically about the youth. "In the Sephardic community there was always a strong sense of tradition," the Rebbe said, "and historically that contributed greatly to their resilient Jewish identity."

The Rebbe then made a personal request of Mr. Cayre. "It's very important to me that you make a recording of the Sephardic High Holiday melodies," the Rebbe said.

"Have the liturgy sung by the very best cantor you can find, so that the children can understand how their parents and grandparents prayed. This will connect the present to the past and the young to the old."

Know where you come from.
That will help determine
where you'll go.

LOVE AND RELATIONSHIPS

IN SEARCH OF THE PERFECT MATE

"Rebbe," a woman said in *yechidut*, "my daughter is struggling to find a good *shidduch*!"

"Does she know what she is looking for in a husband?" the Rebbe asked.

"She sure does," said the woman, proceeding to enumerate every imaginable quality.

"It sounds to me like you're describing at least three different boys," the Rebbe said with a smile.

He's called "the man of your dreams" for a reason.

A LESSON IN LOVE

Before his wedding, a *chasid* asked the Rebbe whether or not he should follow a custom whereby, under the *chupa*, the groom gently steps on the foot of his bride "in order that his voice will be heard in the home."

The Rebbe advised him against following that custom. "A husband should show his wife so much love that there's never an issue of his voice not being heard."

Where there is love, there is respect.

FIRST THINGS FIRST

A sought-after lecturer came to see the Rebbe for a blessing. She was finding it difficult to juggle the roles of mother, daughter, wife, and public speaker, and was concerned that some of her commitments were suffering as a result.

When her turn came to pass by the Rebbe she requested, "I'd like to ask the Rebbe for a blessing that I be a good mother, a good daughter, and a good wife." Her words felt right, as these were the roles she was filling at the time.

"A good wife is the most important," the Rebbe responded gently.

"Yes, yes," the woman replied, a bit distracted.

The Rebbe grew serious as he repeated the point for emphasis: "A good wife is the most important."

Nurture your relationship
with your spouse.
The other relationships
will follow.

A GROWING LOVE

A *shliach* who was stationed in a particularly challenging location once came to see the Rebbe. After he described the difficulties that consumed much of his time and energy, the Rebbe gently asked, "And how is your relationship with your wife?"

The Rebbe then made an unusual request. He asked the *shliach* to write a note describing the dynamics of his marriage and how it was holding up under the stresses of their *shlichut* in the faraway city.

At the end of his note, in which he had elaborated on his wife's many virtues, the *shliach* wrote: "Perhaps I should not have been so profuse in describing my wife's qualities."

The Rebbe crossed out the word 'not,' and underlined the word 'should,' leaving the sentence to read, "I should ~~not~~ have been so profuse in describing my wife's qualities."

The more you dwell on the qualities of your spouse, the stronger your love will become.

TEA TIME

Dr. Ira Weiss, a cardiologist who treated both the Rebbe and his wife, Rebbetzin Chaya Mushka, enjoyed a close relationship with both of them. The Rebbe once shared a personal anecdote with the physician: "The time I devote to have tea with my wife every day is as important to me as the obligation to put on *tefillin* every day."

Like a husband and wife, love and faith go hand in hand.

A VISION OF LOVE

A young woman turned to the Rebbe for his advice. She was contemplating marriage to a young man whose level of Jewish observance was quite different from hers. Did the Rebbe think their relationship was viable?

"Before a couple decides to get married," the Rebbe explained, "the man must have a real understanding of what the woman wants most in her life, and the woman must have a real understanding of what the man wants most in his life. Each must know the other's vision for his or her life, and support it one hundred percent.

"They don't necessarily need to share the exact same vision for their individual lives, but they must genuinely desire that the other person achieve his or her goals.

"When a couple has this bond, then their marriage will be a healthy one."

You don't need to be on the same page, but you should be reading from the same book.

GIVING AND GROWING

A few days before her wedding, a young bride came to see the Rebbe for a blessing.

No sooner than she began speaking did she burst into tears. Sobbing, she told the Rebbe that she wanted to call off the wedding.

"Why is that?" the Rebbe asked.

"I have a terrible temper," the girl explained, "and I have no patience. While we were dating, my groom never saw this side of me, but once we're married it won't take long for him to realize I'm very different from the woman he dated. Instead of marrying and getting divorced, I'd rather not get married to begin with!"

Looking at her warmly, the Rebbe responded: "In my opinion there's no reason to call off the wedding. Every person has limitations, and yours is not uncommon. Besides, patience and self-discipline can be learned and developed."

Then the Rebbe continued, "Please G-d, you will be blessed with energetic children, and they will teach you patience. Until then, I suggest that you volunteer at a children's hospital. This will help you develop patience."

The more we give of ourselves, the more of ourselves we have to give.

TRUE CARING

The Rebbe's wife, Rebbetzin Chaya Mushka, was
suffering from an eye ailment. The *chasid* who arranged for
her to see a specialist asked her, "Did you ask the Rebbe for
a blessing?"

"I didn't," she responded.

"But Rebbetzin," he said respectfully, "people write
to your husband from around the world asking for his
blessing. Why don't you do the same?

"I don't want him to worry," she replied simply.

The *chasid* decided to bring the matter to the
Rebbe himself.

"The Rebbetzin has a problem with one of her eyes,"
he said, "and I've arranged for her to see a specialist. She
doesn't want to mention it, because she doesn't want the
Rebbe to be concerned, so I want to ask you for a blessing on
her behalf!"

The Rebbe said, "Thank you for letting me know about
her condition. I will offer a special prayer for her, but please
don't mention to her that you told me. I don't want her
to be upset."

*Sometimes it's what you don't
say that best expresses
your affection.*

A LOVING PAIN

In an audience with the Rebbe, a man mentioned that his daughter was suffering from a toothache. He requested a blessing that his daughter's pain be eased.

Sometime later, the daughter's husband met with the Rebbe on a different matter. The Rebbe inquired how his wife was doing. Not wanting to trouble the Rebbe with the details, he replied that "it was only a toothache," which, in any case, had already been healed.

The Rebbe grew serious and surprised the young man with his penetrating response:

"Where in your *ketuba* does it say that you may treat your wife's pain lightly?"

And the Rebbe insisted on hearing the exact details of his wife's treatment.

Treat the pain of someone you love as your own.

THE PROPER WAY TO CELEBRATE

During the 1960s, the Rebbe discontinued his practice of officiating at the weddings of *chasidim*. The growing number of weddings, alongside the other pressures on the Rebbe's time, meant that he no longer had room in his schedule.

An individual whose family had known the Rebbe's family in Russia hoped that an exception would be made in his case. He asked the Rebbe to attend his son's *oifruf* celebration, and to share a few words.

The Rebbe replied: "A couple should not begin their new life together by arousing jealousy among their peers."[20]

A celebration should draw others inside, rather than leave them looking on enviously from the outside.

THE PRICE OF FRIENDSHIP

A young man wrote a letter requesting the Rebbe's advice in spiritual matters. After responding to his specific questions, the Rebbe added:

"An important aspect of wellbeing, and one of the greatest gifts in life, is to have a true friend. In *Ethics of the Fathers*, we are taught an important lesson about friendship: 'Designate for yourself a teacher and acquire for yourself a friend.' The word 'acquire,' which the sages use in relation to a friend, teaches the importance of investing time, effort, and energy in creating and maintaining lasting friendships."

> *"A friend sticks closer than a brother."* —PROVERBS[21]

LOVING OR LEARNING

A man once visited the Rebbe to request his advice regarding a relationship. "Rebbe," he said. "I am currently going out with a girl whom I like. But she comes from a far less religious background than my own, and she's much less knowledgeable than I regarding Jewish practice. Can this marriage work?"

The Rebbe responded: "As you describe it, you would need to guide her in those areas of life in which a Jewish woman must be expert. Surely she can be taught, but that's not a healthy role for a husband.

"A wife is not a student and marriage is not a classroom."

> *Marry your spouse for who they are, not for who you'd like them to become.*

START-UP PEDIGREE

A couple sought the Rebbe's advice regarding a possible match for their daughter. They were hesitant because they came from very distinguished lineage, but their potential son-in-law did not.

"Is this a valid reservation?" they asked.

The Rebbe responded: "Would you have refused to take Abraham as your son-in-law? After all, his father, Terah, worshipped idols...."

Pedigree is inherited,
nobility is earned.

FAITH AND PRAYER

DEFINING 'OBSERVANT'

A man came to the Rebbe requesting his blessings for a cousin who had been diagnosed with cancer.

The Rebbe said: "Our sages teach that a person's physical state can be affected by their spiritual condition. Tell me about your cousin's level of observance."

"Well, she's not observant," the man responded.

"Then encourage her to take a *mitzvah* upon herself," the Rebbe said. "Can you suggest, for example, that she begin lighting *Shabbat* candles each Friday night?"

"I believe she already lights *Shabbat* candles," he replied.

As though personally offended, the Rebbe exclaimed, "Then how can you say she isn't observant?"

"The deeper meaning of the word 'mitzvah' is not 'command,' but 'connection.'" —THE ALTER REBBE[22]

DIVINE SPARK

"What do you do?" the Rebbe asked a young man who came to meet with him.

"I'm a student at university," he responded. "I'm studying for a Master's degree in education."

"That's special," the Rebbe said. "I, too, attended university some years ago."

Somewhat surprised, the young man asked, "And what did you study, theology?"

"No, I studied electrical engineering," the Rebbe responded with a smile. "But I prefer to turn the lights on in people's souls."

The Rebbe explained: "You see, every human being has a soul, a divine spark that burns inside them. Sometimes a person moves away from their inner light—it might even seem that the light of their soul has been snuffed out. But the soul is like a pilot light—it never goes out completely. All it needs is for someone to fan the embers with love, until their spiritual fire burns bright again."

"The soul of man is the flame of G-d." —PROVERBS[23]

A LESSON IN MEDICINE

After his wife had been diagnosed with a life-threatening illness, a distraught husband came to see the Rebbe, bringing along his two little children.

"Rebbe," he broke down crying, "I am a sick man who just immigrated to the United States with my family. I don't even know English! And now my wife is going to die, leaving me to care for these two little children!"

"Who said she will die?" the Rebbe asked, visibly upset.

"The doctor," he responded.

"Do you have the prognosis with you?" the Rebbe asked.

"Yes," said the man, handing it to the Rebbe.

The Rebbe took the paper and tore it up.

"Since when do doctors determine who will live and who will die?" he demanded. "Only G-d can do that!"

"Now, go home and tell your wife that she should continue taking her prescribed medication, and she will be fine."

The woman lived for many years.

"Doctors were given permission to heal." —TALMUD[24]

"Only to heal, but not to sow despair."—THE REBBE[25]

SPIRITUAL RECIPE

A Jewish author wanted to understand the essence of the *chasidic* approach to Judaism.

"Let's take bread as a metaphor," the Rebbe began. "Even if you have all the ingredients perfectly arranged, and the dough kneaded to perfection, unless it is placed in a fiery oven for some time, the ingredients will remain just that: ingredients. But you won't have bread!"

The Rebbe elaborated: "The same is true of prayer and the performance of *mitzvot*. One is able to make a blessing by simply saying the words, and doing a *mitzvah* can be merely performing a deed. However, *chasidut* demands that we become an oven—a fiery space created of enthusiasm and passion and joy. That's when *mitzvot* come alive!"

> *"Without love and awe of G-d, a* mitzvah *cannot take flight."* —TANYA[26]

TIMELESS WISDOM

A *yeshiva* student once lent the Rebbe the book, *Perashat Derachim*. After some time had passed and the Rebbe hadn't yet returned the book, the student approached the Rebbe after prayers one day and asked respectfully, "Rebbe, do you no longer need the book *Perashat Derachim*?"

The Rebbe responded warmly, "*Oif ah sefer zogt men nit 'darft nisht'*—When referring to a holy book, we don't use the expression 'no longer need....'"

Holy books provide inspiration, not just information.

BABY STEPS
IN THE RIGHT DIRECTION

"Many Jews today are searching for a way to return to Judaism," a prominent writer told the Rebbe. "What would you say to them to help them find their way?"

The Rebbe paused for a moment. "I would say that the most important thing is not to compromise in their search for the truth. I would refer them to the words of the prophet Elijah: 'How long shall you waver between two opinions? If the L-rd be G-d, follow Him; but if Baal, follow him.' One who tries to decide between faith and the wider environment is unable to go in either direction. He remains unable to distinguish the truth."

"But would not such a person reject such rigid alternatives?" the writer asked.

Replied the Rebbe: "They might have, but for the contribution of *Chasidism*, which teaches that Judaism is really not about 'all or nothing.' Even a small *mitzvah* is an entire world. One can begin the journey by fulfilling one simple *mitzvah*."[27]

Choose a destination.
Get there step by step.

MAKING ALIYA

A man asked the Rebbe whether he should move to Israel to fulfill the Jewish aspiration to leave the *galut*—which means *exile*, or Diaspora.

The Rebbe responded: "What is *galut*? It means the estrangement of an individual from his essence. If someone moves from a hostile environment where he observed the *mitzvot*, and comes to America, for example, where he abandons his beliefs and traditions, he has gone into exile, because he has strayed from his own essence. It's not just assimilation: In English, we call it an 'inferiority complex.' The belief that one's own values are inferior to the values of those around oneself."

Concluded the Rebbe: "If one forsakes their heritage to act like all other nations, then it's possible to be in Israel and still be in *galut*.'"

> *Israel is not just a place on the map, but a place in the heart, mind, and soul.*

INWARD TRAVEL

"I came here to look for some *yiddishkeit*," said a philanthropist who had traveled from overseas to visit the Rebbe.

"You didn't have to come all the way here for that," said the Rebbe. "You only had to look deep inside your own heart."[28]

The inspiration you are seeking is already deep within you.

A CHILD'S PRAYER

In 1950, a man came to pray at the synagogue in "770" together with his six-year-old son.

As the afternoon service was about to commence, the young boy began looking for a prayer book. The prayers had already begun, but the boy was still empty handed.

Making his way back toward his father, he saw another man inviting him to come over to share his *siddur*. This man was none other than the Rebbe, or RaMaSh as he was known at the time, after the initials of his name. The boy sat down next to RaMaSh and together they began to pray from the same *siddur*.

The *chasidim* were uncomfortable with this spectacle, feeling that it was degrading for RaMaSh to pray together with a little boy. They motioned to the bewildered child to return to his father. When RaMaSh realized what was happening, he looked at the well-meaning *chasidim* and said, "What do you want from him? My prayers are proceeding very nicely when he prays with me!"

---

*"If only I could pray
with the innocence of a child."*
—RABBI SHIMSHON OF CHINON[29]

SOUL FOOD

In 1969, the Rebbe read the keynote address delivered
by Mr. Gordon Zacks, a prominent businessman and
politician, to the Council of Jewish Federations. Afterwards,
he invited Mr. Zacks to a private meeting.

"I have read your speech," the Rebbe told Mr. Zacks, "and
it's clear that you've taken good care of your mind. I look at
you, and it's clear that you've taken good care of your body.
What are you doing to take care of your soul?"

*In order to thrive, your soul,
too, needs to be nourished.*

COLLATERAL EFFECT

From the 1940s onwards, Chabad student volunteers began traveling across America, seeking out Jews living in remote towns and farms, isolated from Jewish life. Sometimes, their outreach work bore immediate fruit. And sometimes, they had little or no success.

In the summer of 1955, as a group of students was about to embark on a summer's journey across America, the Rebbe shared a story with them.

"In a small town in America, a Jew looked out of his window and saw a *yeshiva* student pass by. The young bearded man with a *yarmulke* and *tzitzit* caught his attention. 'Where is that young man from? Poland, Galicia, Ukraine?' he asked. 'No,' he was told, 'he's from Boston.'

"The man said: 'A Bostonian! With a beard, side-locks, and *tzitzit*!'

"The *yeshiva* student walking on his way was unaware of his impact upon the man at the window, who was inspired to explore his heritage. The man started by keeping kosher, and little by little began to observe more *mitzvot.* To this very day, the student has no idea what he accomplished!

"One of the highest form of charity is when neither giver nor receiver knows the other's identity. So this was an act of spiritual charity at its best—the student had no idea whom he had influenced, and the man had no idea who had influenced him. There's no telling just how far-reaching the effect will be, and how it will impact the man's children and grandchildren until the end of time.

"In the course of your mission you will teach the Jews whom you meet; but beyond that, you may achieve wonders by your mere presence alone."[30]

> *You may never be fully aware of the impact of your actions.*

EFFECTIVE PRAYER

Mrs. Rochel Fogelman would often write to the Rebbe asking that he pray on behalf of her sister, who was having difficulty finding a *shidduch*, a marriage partner.

On one occasion, Mrs. Fogelman brought a group of students to see the Rebbe. Accompanying them was the mother of one of the students. At the end of the audience, the mother asked if she could speak with the Rebbe privately.

After the meeting with the mother ended, the Rebbe's secretary approached Mrs. Fogelman. "The Rebbe would like to see you."

This was quite unusual, and she was nervous as she entered the Rebbe's room. The Rebbe greeted her with a broad smile and said, "The lady whom you brought to see me today asked for a blessing that her daughter find a suitable *shidduch*. I would like you to take an active interest in her daughter's *shidduch*, and in that merit, I assure you that shortly your sister will find her partner, please G-d."

> *"One who prays on someone else's behalf is answered first."* —THE TALMUD[31]

INSIDE OUT

Deeply invested in the idea of *tikkun olam*, an aspiring activist asked the Rebbe, "Should I focus on making myself better, or should I concentrate solely on changing the world?"

The Rebbe responded, "You cannot fix the world unless you begin with yourself first. Start with yourself, then your family, then your community, then your country and from there, the world: one step at a time."

> *If you nurture your own fire,*
> *its warmth will spread*
> *to those around you.*

TRUST IN G-D

Moshe Mendel visited the Rebbe and complained, "Rebbe, no matter what I do, I am unable to provide for my wife and four children!"

The Rebbe replied, "The Talmud teaches that G-d sits on His Heavenly throne each day and 'supports and sustains the whole world, from the horns of the reindeer to the eggs of lice.'"

The conversation then turned to Moshe Mendel's past. He had lost his mother at a young age, and was mistreated terribly by his stepmother. By virtue of a blessing he received from the Belzer Rebbe he avoided being drafted into the Polish army. He was later drafted into the Russian army, but through a series of extraordinary circumstances he survived, escaped the Nazis, married, and miraculously arrived on American shores.

After telling the Rebbe the incredible story of his survival, Mendel again brought up his financial woes.

"But didn't we just decide that G-d will provide for your

livelihood?" the Rebbe asked. "Don't you trust in Him?"

"If I didn't trust in G-d, would I be here?" Moshe asked. "In fact, before coming to you, I visited all the Rebbes who would meet with me. Doesn't that demonstrate my faith in G-d?"

"With all due respect," the Rebbe said, "that demonstrates your faith in Rebbes, not in G-d.

"When you related the incredible story of how you survived," the Rebbe noted gently, "you didn't mention G-d even once. It seems to me that ever since you met the Belzer Rebbe and experienced miracles, you began to believe in Rebbes, rather than believing in G-d. Now let us work to change that."[32]

*Don't confuse the agent of a blessing
with its source.*

THE CHASIDIC WORLDVIEW

As Passover neared, a benefactor paid for free suits for the *yeshiva* students at "770." The young men visited a store on the Lower East Side to choose their new clothes.

The next day the Rebbe spotted a young student who was new to the *yeshiva* in the hallway, wearing an oversized and ill-fitting suit. "Tell me," the Rebbe asked with concern, "are you eating well? Have you lost weight recently? I'm asking because your suit, though very nice, seems a bit big on you."

The young man replied, "Everything is alright, thank G-d. I actually got this suit only yesterday.

"But what difference does it make if my suit is a size too big or too small?" the enthusiastic student continued. "It's only *gashmiut*, materialism. It's got nothing to do with the important things in life, the spiritual."

The Rebbe responded earnestly, "*Chasidism* is not asceticism—the belief that self-denial is the pathway to G-d. On the contrary, *chasidism* teaches that every aspect of one's physical existence can be channeled into the service of G-d."

*Like horse and rider, body and soul
are meant to be a team.*

AN EXQUISITE MITZVAH

A businessman brought an antique silver *menorah* as a gift to the Rebbe. It was handmade and amazingly intricate, adorned with sculptured silver lions whose mouths opened to reveal candle wicks for lighting.

Fascinated by its unique design, the Rebbe spent several minutes studying the beautiful artistry, complimenting the businessman for his thoughtful gift.

Then he continued gently, "I'm sorry, but I'll have to decline your gift. The *menorah* I use is a gift from someone else, who will be hurt if I begin using a different one."

> A mitzvah *is only as beautiful as the sensitivity with which it is performed.*

A LIVING EXAMPLE

After years of trying, a *chasid* succeeded in securing a meeting with a renowned Jewish professor, with the hope of drawing him closer to *yiddishkeit*. When he was finally admitted to the professor's office, the *chasid* realized that it was getting dark and it would soon be too late to recite the afternoon prayer. In the middle of their discussion, as the professor turned away to look up a reference, the rabbi turned around, faced the wall, and began to pray.

The professor was stunned. He had never seen anyone pray in an office. To his knowledge, prayer was offered during a formal service, in a temple, and at a designated time. That someone should pray in the midst of his much-anticipated meeting intrigued him, and he was deeply moved.

A relationship developed between the two, and that meeting became the first of many to come.

The Rebbe told the story at a *farbrengen*, drawing a lesson from the episode:

"Although the two men delved into Jewish philosophy and Torah's view on many aspects of life, it was the *chasid's* simple afternoon prayer that changed the professor's life. That prayer opened the door for the professor to view G-d from a totally new perspective."[33]

Actions speak louder than any words.

THE SECRET OF AMERICAN JEWS

During a visit with the Rebbe in the 1950s, a leading author commented on the sad state of American Jewry.

The Rebbe replied: "Many religious people have despaired on the future of American Jewry, given their present level of their Torah observance.

"I, however, am *upbeat* about American Jewry. While you cannot *tell* them to do anything, you can *teach* them to do everything!"

In a world governed by choice,
wisdom must be offered, not imposed.

JEWISH LEADERSHIP

RULES OF DISENGAGEMENT

A man who had worked as a school principal for many years was experiencing difficulties at his job. He decided the time had come to resign.

He traveled to New York and, upon entering the Rebbe's study shortly after midnight, he unburdened himself, expressing his desire to finally walk away from the difficulties of running the school.

After hearing him out, the Rebbe asked, "And who do you think will replace you?"

"I don't know," the man responded, somewhat sheepishly.

"My father-in-law would say that the hour from 12 to one in the morning is *'a narishe sha'a*—a silly hour," replied the Rebbe, with a twinkle in his eye. "But such *narishkayt*, I never expected!"

If you don't provide another way,
it's wrong to step away.

'AMAZING' DEFINED

Standing in line to meet the Rebbe one Sunday, the successful businessman Gordon Zacks reflected that 18 years had passed since he had last seen the Rebbe.

When his turn came, he approached the Rebbe, who looked at him with smiling eyes. Picking up their conversation exactly where they had left off 18 years earlier, the Rebbe said, "I hope you won't wait this long to come back again and report good news in your work for Jewish education!"

The Rebbe had met hundreds of thousands of people over the course of those years. Astounded by the Rebbe's extraordinary memory, Zacks exclaimed: "Wow! Rebbe, you are amazing. That was 18 years ago!"

Without skipping a beat, the Rebbe responded: "And what will be the benefit to the community that I am 'amazing?'"

*Leadership is measured
not by personal virtue, but by
the benefit brought to others.*

A NOBLE DIVERSION

It was reported to the Rebbe that a member of a particular community was a constant source of conflict.

The Rebbe asked to see one of the lay leaders of the community, telling him, "I suggest that you give this individual a communal position. For example, appoint him to be the *gabai*, warden, of the synagogue. Keep him busy."

The Rebbe continued, "In Petersburg, my father-in-law, the Rebbe Rayatz, once called me into his office and told me that so-and-so—an individual known for his contentious personality—was coming to town, and was likely to stir up conflict.

"'Please see to it that he is kept busy,' he told me, 'so that he stays out of trouble.'

"'In Petersburg,' my father-in-law continued with a smile, 'there's a big monument of Czar Alexander in front of the train station. The Czar was a tall, strapping man and the huge sculpture depicts him riding on a large stallion. In front of this imposing monument a soldier always stood guard.

"A person coming from the train station once asked a bystander, 'Tell me, why do they need a soldier to guard this monument? Who could possibly steal this enormous statue?'

The fellow responded, 'Look, as long as the soldier stands here, at least the soldier himself is not stealing!'"

"I don't ask of my chasidim *not to sin, I ask of them not to have time to sin."* —REB MENDEL OF KOTZK

STOKING THE FIRE

During a *Shabbat* afternoon *farbrengen* at "770," a group of visiting women were singing along in the women's balcony.

A man rushed over to the Rebbe: "Jewish law forbids women from singing in the presence of men! Should I send them a message to stop singing?"

"No," replied the Rebbe with a smile, "don't *stop* their singing. Instead, ask the women to please *add* to the joy of the *farbrengen* by clapping enthusiastically!"

Channel a fire of inspiration.
If you snuff it out,
it might never be rekindled.

MACROMANAGEMENT

Rabbi Nachman and Fradel Sudak were among the Rebbe's first *shluchim*. Before moving to England, they visited the Rebbe privately.

"Rebbe, what are we supposed to do when we arrive to England?" the couple asked. "In what areas should we concentrate our energy? Please give us some direction."

The Rebbe responded, "When you get there you will see that there are thousands of things to do. Based on your findings there, *you* will choose the projects that are most suitable."

A true leader creates leaders, not followers.

LIFE-COACH

Herbert Weiner, author of *Nine-and-a-Half Mystics*, asked the Rebbe: "How do you assume responsibility for giving advice to people on all matters, not only religious, but on business and medical matters also, especially when you know that your advice is often binding?"

The Rebbe replied: "When a person comes with a problem there are only two alternatives—either send him away, or try to help him. A man knows his own problem best, so one must try to unite oneself with him and become as dissociated as possible from one's own ego. Then, in concert with the other person, one tries to understand the rule of Divine Providence in his particular case."[34]

> *Before transmitting the music in your soul, help others hear the music in theirs.*

A LESSON IN LEADERSHIP

In 1964, when Robert F. Kennedy was running for U.S. Senate in New York, he visited the Rebbe for a private audience. During their conversation, the Rebbe brought up a topic that was close to his heart: financial aid for tax-paying families who were struggling to pay tuition for their children in private schools.

As he explained why he couldn't support government aid for such schools, Kennedy began with a disclaimer:

"You know, I'm a Catholic, and I have eight children of my own…"

The Rebbe interjected, "Yes, but I have two hundred thousand."[35]

A true leader considers every constituent their child.

A JEWISH HALLMARK

A Jewish leader visited the Rebbe to discuss his concern at the alarming rate of Jewish assimilation. The Rebbe confided: "It pains me that when one Jew helps another to put on *tefillin*, people say, 'Oh, he must be a Lubavitcher.'

"I look forward to the day when providing *mitzvah* opportunities to our less knowledgeable brethren will no longer be a hallmark of Lubavitch, but of every observant Jew."

If your objective is the end result, you don't have to corner the market.

THE GOLDEN RULE

In 1962, the Rebbe sent Rabbi Moshe and Mindy Feller on
shlichus to Minnesota. They did not have a rabbinical post or
a faculty position awaiting them. They were moving there
as grassroots activists with the aim of bringing Jews closer
to Judaism. In a private audience with the Rebbe, Rabbi
Feller asked, "Rebbe, what should we do when we get there?
Where should we begin, and what should our strategy be?"

The Rebbe responded, "I can't give you any specific
instructions, but I can tell you this: Be flexible and don't get
stuck in your ways. Always remain sensitive to the needs of
the people there."

*Is it about your vision
or their needs?*

THE LONG-SHORT WAY

A Chabad couple moved to a remote location, in the hope of sharing the beauty of *yiddishkeit* with their brethren.

Initially, they struggled to make inroads into the local community. One time, the *shlucha* was invited to give a lecture in a private home. Her audience was so impressed with her remarks that they asked her to share more insights right then and there. However, the *shlucha's* mind drew a blank. Mortified, she had to decline the offer.

On the train ride home, she could not stop crying, distraught by the missed opportunity. A few days passed, and she was still feeling dejected. She wrote to the Rebbe, expressing her disappointment.

The Rebbe responded: "*Chasidic* literature describes the difference between 'seeding' and 'planting.' When one sows wheat, the product grows quite quickly. When one plants a seed, however, it takes quite some time before a fruit grows.

"The efforts of a human being are much the same. Never mind the incident at the class. If your effort doesn't bear immediate results, you might be engaged in 'planting,' where the ultimate reward might take longer to materialize, but will be infinitely greater."[36]

> *Don't judge yourself*
> *by immediate results. There are no*
> *shortcuts to any place worth going.*

A WISE INVESTMENT

A Chabad *chasid* who was a successful businessman was invited to an audience with the Rebbe.

The Rebbe told him that a newspaper affiliated with the conservative stream of Judaism was having financial difficulties. "Please contact the management," said the Rebbe. "Without telling them who sent you, find out how much money is needed to keep them in operation, and let me know the figure. I would like to help keep the paper running."

Surprised, the *chasid* thought: "That newspaper? They are opposed to traditional *halacha*!"

As if reading the *chasid's* thoughts, the Rebbe continued: "This paper reaches thousands of Jews. Every Friday they print the weekly *Shabbat* candle lighting time, as well as the time that *Shabbat* ends. If the paper folds, thousands of Jewish women may not know the *Shabbat* candle lighting times, and what time *Shabbat* concludes."

Put deed before creed.

A MORAL REVOLUTION

Rabbi Dr. Israel Drazin served as Brigadier General and Assistant Chief of Chaplains of the U.S. Army for over three decades. At the Rebbe's suggestion, Drazin made considerable efforts to increase awareness of the Seven Noahide Laws, moral imperatives shared by Jews and non-Jews.

In a 1986 letter, the Rebbe wrote to him: "There is, of course, no need to emphasize the importance of promoting these Seven Noahide Commandments among Gentiles. It does not require much imagination to realize that had these Divine Commandments been observed and adhered to by all the 'Children of Noah,' namely, the nations of the world, individually and collectively, there would not have been any possibility in the natural order of things for such a thing as the Holocaust."

Teaching morality is the way to turn "Never again!" from slogan to reality.

FIRST IMPRESSIONS

A teacher brought a group of 50 *yeshiva* students to meet with the Rebbe. The teacher encouraged the students to contribute a single dollar along with their private notes to the Rebbe, to be donated to one of the Rebbe's charitable organizations.

As they entered the Rebbe's room, the teacher handed over an envelope containing the 50 dollars he had collected from his students, while the boys each handed over their personal notes. After the Rebbe addressed them, the students left the room while their teacher stayed on to discuss some personal matters.

At the end of their conversation, the Rebbe gently admonished the teacher for collecting money from his young charges:

"The students might walk away with the impression that everything is about money, even if the money is for charity. In their minds, religious leaders might become associated with taking, rather than giving. Your students must know that a Rebbe, and by extension all of their teachers and leaders, is here to give, not to take."

"You shall choose out of the entire nation men of substance, G-d fearers, men of truth, who hate monetary gain, and you shall appoint them leaders..." —EXODUS[37]

THE BOTTOM LINE

The manager of a *gemach*, or free loan society, visited the Rebbe to discuss his organization. He presented the Rebbe with a report of the *gemach's* income and expenses for that year. He proudly pointed to the substantial balance in the account, reflecting the *gemach's* fundraising and administrative capabilities.

The Rebbe responded, "A successful free loan society is defined not by how much money it brings in, but by how much money it lends out. You should see to it that from now on all of your *gemach's* monies are constantly lent out."

A successful business is measured by how much it brings in. A successful charity is measured by how much it gives out.

EXPONENTIAL GROWTH

A new rabbi on university campus was feeling overwhelmed by the magnitude of his role. "Rebbe," he asked during a *yechidut*, "How am I, one individual, supposed to reach the 7,000 Jewish students who attend my university?!"

The Rebbe responded: "Your job is not to work with 7,000. Your job is to work with seven. Those seven will reach another seven, who in turn will reach another seven, *ad infinitum*."

Quality begets quantity.

OTHER-CENTERED

A wealthy man asked the Rebbe's advice on how to be a better Jew.

The Rebbe told him, "Although it's important to work on self-refinement, the call of the hour is to better the lives of others.

"Let me tell you a story: A great Jewish sage was asked for a substantial donation by a person in need. The rabbi went straight to his drawer, took out his savings and gave the entire amount to the poor man. When the rabbi's wife realized what he had done, she was very upset, exclaiming, 'What have you done? You've given away all of our savings!'

"The rabbi responded, 'My dear wife, last night I dreamt that I had passed away. When I arrived at the Gates of Heaven, a renowned Torah scholar was waiting to enter. After some time, it was confirmed by the Heavenly court that he had spent his lifetime in the study of G-d's wisdom, but he was not admitted immediately.

"'Then another soul came along. His passion in life had been giving *tzedaka*. It was established that he had devoted most of his energies to helping others. The Gates of Heaven swung open immediately, and he was allowed into *Gan Eden*.'

"Of all the worthy pursuits one can get involved in," the Rebbe concluded, "acts of giving have the most merit in the eyes of Hashem."

> *Improving the world around us comes before perfecting our own inner world.*

A RELEVANT GIFT

A group of Chabad emissaries from across Canada arranged to meet with Canadian Prime Minister Brian Mulroney.

They had purchased a beautiful silver *kiddush* cup to present to the Prime Minister as a gift. The emissaries planned to explain to the Prime Minister that every human being, especially a government leader, has the ability to "make *kiddush*"—to sanctify his or her surroundings.

The day before the meeting, Rabbi Zalman Aaron Grossbaum, a senior *shliach* in Canada, wrote to the Rebbe telling him of their planned appointment with the Prime Minister and the gift they had readied.

The Rebbe's response proved enlightening.

"Of what use is a *kiddush* cup to the Prime Minister? I would suggest, instead, that you present him with an English prayer book, as it includes prayers such as *Modeh Ani*—a prayer recited each morning thanking G-d for giving us life—which are relevant and meaningful to non-Jews, as well."

Make sure every encounter has the utmost meaning.

A CALL TO ACTION

A writer researching a book about great Jewish scholars and leaders mentioned an important figure during a conversation with the Rebbe.

"He was a wonderful man," the Rebbe commented, before his voice trailed off.

"What is it?" the writer prodded.

"Well," answered the Rebbe, "if there were one critique I would offer, it would be that his writings lack '*tachlis*,' a bottom line or focused points of action. His followers are left unsure how to act upon the knowledge and inspiration he imparted."

When a great speaker finishes talking, his audience erupts to applause. When a great leader finishes talking his audience exclaims: "Let's march!"

LIFETIME COMMITMENT

A renowned rabbi who decided it was time to retire shared his plans with the Rebbe.

"Retirement?" the Rebbe asked incredulously. "Not for a rabbi! Someone who has led others his entire life develops the need to guide and inspire for as long as he lives. Depriving him of an outlet to share is like depriving him of life itself."[38]

*Strive to reach the level
where giving is living.*

WINNING THE RACE

A young couple moved to a town and established a Jewish day school. After years of hard work they began to see the fruits of their labor. But their new success drew the attention of some members of the local Jewish establishment, who felt threatened by their accomplishments. "Who gave you the right to open up institutions in the first place?" they demanded. "And besides, your success will be short-lived. Why put in all this effort when you will not be able to sustain it?"

Disheartened, the couple sought out the Rebbe's counsel and encouragement.

After hearing of their distress and self-doubt, the Rebbe responded with a story: "Rabbi Yonatan Eibshitz, the 18th century scholar, was well-liked by the governor of his area.

"The anti-Semitic ministers, however, tried to undermine the relationship, maligning the rabbi at every opportunity.

"One day, the governor decided to put an end to the simmering conflict between the rabbi and the ministers.

He summoned them all, informing them that he would

hold a competition to determine who among them was superior: A chicken race.

"The owner of the chicken who reached the finish-line first would be the champion in the battle underway at the governor's court.

"Needless to say, the ministers fed their roosters well. On the day of the competition, they presented their fat, strong, chickens at the starting line. Reb Yonatan, however, showed up with a scrawny little chicken.

"The race was on. In the midst of the contest, the plumped-up roosters began to fight with each other. They scratched and tussled aggressively, completely ignoring Rabbi Yonatan's gaunt and haggard little chicken. The puny bird who didn't seem to stand a chance, inched its way across the finish line first."

If you stay focused,
you can defy expectations.

WHERE TO LIVE

An observant couple living in Minnesota wrote to the Rebbe, requesting his advice as to whether they should move to New York or stay in Minneapolis. "It's much easier to live a religious Jewish life in New York," they wrote.

The Rebbe advised them to remain, because, "New York has many observant Jews already; in Minneapolis your presence will have a much greater impact."

Where can you have the most impact?

A SPIRITUAL EQUATION

In 1986, the Rebbe instituted a practice known as
"Sunday Dollars." The Rebbe, who was then in his 84th year,
would receive people from all walks of life at "770." Young
and old, statesmen, laymen, Jews from all backgrounds,
as well as many Gentiles attended. They waited on line for
hours to exchange a few words with the Rebbe and receive
his blessing, before receiving a dollar bill to be given to a
charity of their choice.

When the philanthropist Ronald Lauder reached the
front of the line, the Rebbe explained the practice: "When
two people meet, something good should result for a third."

*In a spiritual encounter
one plus one equals three.*

THE BEST NEIGHBORHOOD

A much respected rabbi, with many years of outstanding service in prestigious congregations across America, retired and moved to Bnei Brak in Israel, a city with a large observant population. In an audience with the Rebbe, the gentleman's son, himself a respected rabbi, mentioned his father's recent move.

"He blends in there, and he can study Torah to his heart's content," the son explained.

The Rebbe responded, "I think it's a mistake for him to live there."

"Why?" the son asked in surprise.

"Your father was a much respected rabbi in the States, the spiritual leader of many communities. In Bnei Brak, no one knows him and he will not be treated with the respect he deserves. He'll just be another Jew with a beard."

"So where does the Rebbe recommend that he live?" the son asked.

"He should move to Tel Aviv, where he can bring his talents to bear. There he would make a difference and be respected and appreciated."

*Part of what makes us human
is our longing to feel needed
and heeded.*

FILLING OUT THE POSITION

The Rebbe once encouraged a *chasid* to pursue a challenging leadership position in Australia. The *chasid's* wife, who was present at the meeting, was outspoken in her objection. "How can he take this position when he clearly doesn't have the background necessary to fill it?" She was worried that her husband might be setting himself up for disappointment and embarrassment.

The Rebbe smiled in appreciation and understanding, and replied, "When it is meant to be, the position makes the man."

No man is born great.
Rise to the challenge

E PLURIBUS UNUM—FROM MANY, ONE

In the wake of the Crown Heights riots of 1991, David Dinkins, the mayor of New York City, visited the Rebbe one Sunday afternoon to receive a dollar and a blessing for peace between "the two groups"—the Jewish and black residents of the neighborhood.

The Rebbe responded, "Not two peoples and two sides, but one people and one side."

> *The first step towards reconciliation is finding the other within oneself.*

SHIFTING FOCUS

Rabbi Chaskel Besser, a prominent American rabbi and a Holocaust survivor, worked for Polish Jewry on behalf of the Ronald S. Lauder Foundation. He traveled frequently to Poland in order to rebuild and preserve Jewish cemeteries in his native country.

Besser shared a close relationship with the Rebbe, and would often consult with him. One Sunday afternoon when her husband was on a trip to Poland, Mrs. Besser went to "770" to see the Rebbe.

"Where is your husband today?" the Rebbe asked.

"He's in Europe, working on restoring the *batei chaim*," she replied, using the Hebrew euphemism referring to a cemetery as a "place of the living."

"Please tell your husband that he should work not only with the *batei chaim* for those who have passed, but with the '*chaim*'—the living—as well."

The best way to honor those who have passed is to devote yourself to those who are present.

A REPRESENTATIVE'S STATUS

When the Chief Rabbi of Romania came to meet with the Rebbe, he noticed many people waiting for a private audience. After a few minutes with the Rebbe, he started to draw their conversation to a close. "I don't want to take up too much of your time," he said.

The Rebbe replied with a question: "How many Jews are there in Romania?"

"Sixty-thousand," the rabbi answered.

"Then we have as much time as is necessary for sixty-thousand Jews."

If you represent a community, don't be humble on their behalf.

FIRST AID

In the late 1960s, a Jewish chaplain on a college campus turned to the Rebbe for advice. "Many of my Jewish students are involved in social causes, and I'm unsure to what extent I should invest myself in their projects, especially since it is taking a toll on the Jewish programming I arrange for Jewish students."

The Rebbe responded poignantly: "You have a responsibility to help every human being, and you should therefore help anyone who is in pain. At the same time, you must consider the priorities presented to you by your current reality."

"If two people are drowning and you have the ability to save only one of them, and one is your brother and one is a stranger, would anyone take issue if you saved your brother first?"

"If and when you've fulfilled your obligations to your brethren, you can continue with your other priorities to strangers. But you must focus on your own first."

"The poor of your city come first."
—TALMUD[39]

RIPPLE EFFECT

The Rebbe was speaking with a prominent leader of the
United Jewish Appeal. The subject was a global project the
man had initiated to improve the state of Jews around the
world. After listening to his ambitious idea, the Rebbe said,
"Remember, if you really want to change the world, change
yourself first!

"It's like dropping a stone into a pool of water and
watching the concentric circles radiate to the shore. If you
strengthen your connection to G-d and behave in a manner
which reflects that connection, those around you will be
impacted by your example and they, in turn, will influence
others. Remember to focus on yourself first."

*If you want to affect the world,
change yourself first.*

HIGHLY UNORTHODOX

In her letter to the Rebbe, a woman used the term 'Orthodox Judaism.'

In his response, the Rebbe wrote:

"I must point out to you that splitting Judaism into 'orthodox, conservative, and reform' is a purely artificial division, for all Jews share one and the same Torah given by the One and same G-d. While there are more observant Jews and less observant ones, to tack on a label does not change the reality that we are all one."

Labels create barriers,
turning brothers into 'others.'

HEED YOUR CALLING

A young rabbi who was about to become a practicing psychiatrist came to speak to the Rebbe regarding his career. The Rebbe suggested that he move to New York, so that he could service members of the local Jewish community in need of his help. He protested: "But if I am the only religious psychiatrist in New York, the workload will be so immense, I may never have time to study Torah again!"

Acknowledging his rabbinic background, the Rebbe sensitively but firmly pushed back, citing a *halachic* principle, "A good deed that can only be performed by you takes priority over Torah study."

Are you the only one who can do it? That's G-d's way of saying, "This is yours to pursue."

· ACKNOWLEDGEMENTS ·

I've been enamored by stories for as long as I can remember. Some people are audio learners, some learn through images. But for me, it's about stories; I learn best when a point is made through a narrative, especially an inspirational one.

A story is not a sermon, but a setting. A story shows, rather than tells. From the static, abstract, and theoretical, a truism suddenly comes to life through a real person, a relevant situation, and an actual event. And that is how this book of living wisdom was intended to read. But for that to happen, it became clear to me that the stories could not be grounded upon hearsay, or merely be "based upon a true story."

This, in turn, led me to the archives of the My Encounter with the Rebbe project which, to date, contain the firsthand testimonies of over 800 people describing their personal encounters with the Rebbe. These interviews are the first-person source for this book, and their contribution to the historical accuracy of data relating to the Rebbe cannot be overstated. In many ways, these accounts enabled me to go back in time and personally take part in those very encounters with the Rebbe.

I am deeply grateful to Rabbi Elkanah Shmotkin, the visionary behind Jewish Educational Media (JEM) and its driving force. In addition to founding the *My Encounter with the Rebbe* project and serving as its inspirational guide, Rabbi Shmotkin's stubborn attention to detail—in matters of content, as well as aesthetics—has helped make this book what it is. His vast experience and expertise in interpreting and presenting the Rebbe and his teachings were invaluable.

Rabbi Yechiel Cagen, director of the *My Encounter with the Rebbe* project, is responsible for recording much of the testimony cited here. He graciously assisted me with access to the archives.

It goes without saying that working with firsthand accounts comes with its own set of challenges. There is a delicate balancing act between content and form, authenticity and accessibility—between staying true to the sometimes fragmented accounts of an interviewee, while presenting a smooth and structured read. At times, I felt compelled to take the liberty of completing unfinished thoughts and half sentences, and in so doing, I faced the daunting risks that flow from subjective interpretation. Even letters or talks of the Rebbe have been modified slightly to match the form of this book. Though I tried my best to render each story and quote faithfully, if I came up short, the fault lies with me. Equally, any errors of transmission are my own.

The stories have been reviewed by Rabbis Mendel Feller and Mendel Alperowitz, whose keen and discerning reading ensured that the stories remained true to their sources and to the historical record. I'd like to thank Mr. Ben Cohen and Mrs. Esther Tauber for their expert editing, and Mrs. Sheina Herz for her skilled proofreading.

Thank you to Chanie Kaminker of Hannabi Creative, and Annita Soble for the beautiful layout and cover design.

On a personal note, I would like to dedicate this book to my wife and life partner, Chanale, whose unwavering support and clear thinking has helped bring this project into being. To borrow Rabbi Akiva's words to his students about his wife, Rachel: "What is mine and what is yours, is truly hers."

Additionally, I'd like to express an overwhelming debt of gratitude to my dear parents, Rabbi Yosef Yitzchak and Hindy Kalmenson, and to my beloved grandparents, Rabbi Sholom Ber and Mrs. Sara Shanowitz, and Rabbi Yekusiel Kalmenson of blessed memory and Mrs. Batsheva

Kalmenson, may she live and be well. They have always been a source of constant counsel, support, and love, and have transmitted their profound passion for *yiddishkeit* to their adoring children and grandchildren who, in turn, endeavor to do the same.

Finally, I'd like to express a profound debt of gratitude to the individual at the heart of these stories, the Rebbe, of righteous memory, himself. His example and teachings have helped shape my worldview and life's work, and continue to guide me daily, never ceasing to demand that I be the best and truest version of myself that I can be.

—MENDEL KALMENSON

· ABOUT THE AUTHOR ·

Rabbi Mendel Kalmenson has authored numerous
articles and essays on Jewish thought for Chabad.org.
He lives in London with his family, where he is the rabbi
and executive director of Chabad Belgravia.

• ENDNOTES •

1. *Hayom Yom, 10 Shevat.*
2. *Talmud Kidushin, 56b.*
3. *Midrash Kohelet Rabba, 1:13.*
4. *Psalms, 133:1.*
5. *Talmud Nedarim, 8b.*
6. *Job, 5:7.*
7. *Maimonides Laws of Charity, 10:7.*
8. *Talmud Kidushin, 30b.*
9. *Proverbs 13:24.*
10. *Bereishit Rabba, 84:8.*
11. *Igrot Kodesh vol 18, 222-223.*
12. *Proverbs, 22:6.*
13. *Talmud Sanhedrin, 19b.*
14. *Midrash Bereishit Rabba, 1:1.*
15. *Ethics of the Fathers, 4:20.*
16. *Avoda Zara 19a.*
17. *Song of Songs 1:6.*
18. *Talmud Shavuot 39a.*
19. *Ethics of the Fathers, 1:17.*
20. *Talmud Bava Metzia 42a.*
21. *Proverbs, 18:24.*
22. *Torah Ohr, Genesis 6b.*
23. *Proverbs 20:27.*
24. *Talmud Bava Kama, 85a.*
25. *Igrot Kodesh vol. 4, 288.*
26. *Tanya ch. 41.*
27. *Nine-and-a-Half Mystics, 194-195.*
28. *Challenge, JEM.*
29. *Shaalot Uteshuvot Harivash ch. 157.*
30. *Living Torah Disc 90, Program 357, Sicha segment.*
31. *Talmud Bava Kama 92a.*
32. *Talmud Bava Kama, 92b.*
33. *Hisvaaduyot 5745 vol. 3, 1650.*
34. *Nine-and-a-Half Mystics, 176.*
35. *Sichot Kodesh 5725, vol. 1 530.*
36. *Letter dated 18 Adar II, 5725.*
37. *Exodus 18:21.*
38. *Pesachim 112b.*
39. *Talmud Bava Metzia, 71a.*

· SOURCES ·

Mr. Robert Abrams, *January 21, 2002.*

Rabbi Shabsi Alpern, *November 8, 2010.*

Rabbi Mordechai Altein, *December 29, 2005.*

Rabbi Binyomin Althaus, *March 21, 2012.*

Ambassador Yehuda Avner, *December 29, 2006.*

Mr. Koppel Bacher, *November 8, 2011.*

Rabbi Nachman Bernhard, *January 17, 2011.*

Rabbi Chaskel Besser, *May 13, 2005.*

Mrs. Rivkah Blau, *May 8, 2007.*

Rabbi Dr. Herbert Bomzer, *June 11, 2009.*

Mrs. Hadassah Carlebach, *December 13, 2007.*

Mr. Joseph Cayre, *January 14, 2007.*

Rabbi Hirsch Chitrik, *January 14, 2009.*

Rabbi Chaim Ciment, *June 24, 2007.*

Mrs. Sterna Citron, *September 12, 2011.*

Rabbi Ahron Cousin, *August 9, 2007.*

Mr. Murray Dalfin, *February 16, 2011.*

Mr. Naftali Deutsch, *September 11, 2011.*

Rabbi Dr. Israel Drazin, *March 30, 2011.*

Rabbi Meilech Leib DuBrow, *September 8, 2011.*

Rabbi Mordechai Einbinder, *September 6, 2011.*

Rabbi Chaim Farro, *February 14, 2012.*

Rabbi Hershel Feigelstock, *July 13, 2010.*

Mr. Samuel Feiglin, *December 12, 2006.*

Mr. Moshe Mendel Feiner, *May 12, 2011.*

Rabbi Moshe Feller, *November 28, 2005.*

Mrs. Miriam Fellig, *March 22, 2011.*

Professor Reuven Feuerstein, *July 26, 2011.*

Rabbi Hershel Fogelman, *July 21, 2008.*

· SOURCES ·

Mrs. Rochel Fogelman, *July 21, 2008.*
Mrs. Bassie Garelik, *January 19, 2009.*
Mrs. Esther Goldman, *May 12, 2007.*
Rabbi Moishe Goldman, *March 20, 2011.*
Rabbi Shimon Goldman, *May 12, 2007.*
Mr. Marvin Goldsmith, *August 25, 2012.*
Rabbi Yosef Goldstein, *August 14, 2001.*
Rabbi Joshua Gordon, *September 5, 2011.*
Rabbi Yisroel Gordon, *May 15, 2005.*
Mr. Mendel Greenbaum, *March 31, 2011.*
Professor Velvl Greene, *April 1, 2008.*
Rabbi Yitzchak Maier Gurary, *April 22, 2011.*
Mr. Freddy Hager, *August 9, 2007.*
Professor Susan Handelman, *March 20, 2007.*
Professor Yaakov Hanoka, *March 8, 2008.*
Mrs. Hindy Lew, *August 8, 2007.*
Rabbi Shmuel Lew, *November 28, 2005.*
Rabbi Shmuel Lew, *January 7, 2009.*
Rabbi Raphael Pelcovitz, *October 21, 2010.*
Prime Minister Yitzhak Rabin, *January 3, 1992.*
Rabbi Dr. Jonathan Sacks, *November 7, 2007.*
Rabbi Zev Segal, *May 13, 2007.*
Rabbi Ephraim Sturm, *October 20, 2007.*
Rabbi Nachman Sudak, *August 13, 2007.*
Rabbi Marvin Tokayer, *December 8, 2010.*
Rabbi Norbert Weinberg, *January 28, 2013.*
Rabbi Dr. Laibl Wolf, *November 16, 2008.*
Mr. Gordon Zacks, *August 23, 2007.*

· GLOSSARY ·

770: Shorthand for 770 Eastern Parkway, the address of Chabad's world headquarters in Brooklyn, New York.

Aleph: The first letter of the Hebrew alphabet, known as the *Aleph-Bet.*

Batei chaim: Plural for *beit hachaim,* "place of the living," a euphemism referring to a cemetery.

Chabad: The *chasidic* movement also known as 'Lubavitch.' An acronym for *chachma, bina, daat,* "wisdom, understanding and knowledge," in Hebrew, representing the philosophy of the movement founded by Rabbi Schneur Zalman of Liadi.

Chasid/chasidic/chasidism: Derived from the Hebrew word for 'pious,' a follower chasidism, the Movement founded by Rabbi Israel Baal Shem Tov (1698- 1760). *Chasidism* refers to the movement's philosophy. A *chasid* approaches the commandments of Judaism with intense joy.

Chupa: The canopy underneath which Jewish weddings take place.

Farbrengen/farbrenging: An informal chasidic gathering where friends encourage and assist one-another to improve their relationships with G-d and their contemporaries. In the case of the Rebbe's *farbrengen,* the event has the face of a public address and Torah discourse, bookended by chasidic melodies and toasts of *L'chaim!*

Gabai: Caretaker of a synagogue.

Galut: The exile of the Jewish people after the destruction of the Holy Temples in Jerusalem. Also used to refer to the Diaspora, any location outside of the Holy Land.

Gan Eden: The Garden of Eden, place of reward after life in this world.

Gemach: A fund offering interest-free loans, in accordance with Judaism's prohibition against charging interest.

Haggada: Liturgy of the Passover feast known as the 'seder.'

Halacha/halachic: Torah law.

Ketuba: The Hebrew term for a Jewish contract of marriage.

Kiddush: Derived from the Hebrew term for "sanctification," this is the blessing traditionally recited over wine during Sabbaths and Jewish holidays.

Mame lashon: "Mother tongue," a euphemism for the Yiddish language.

Mazal: A quintessential Yiddish term referring to 'luck,' but for which there is no true translation into English.

Mensch: Literally, 'person,' in Yiddish.

Mishneh Torah: Maimonides' *Magnum Opus*, the first formal codification of Jewish law.

Mitzvah/mitzvot: The Hebrew word for "commandment," refers to the 613 commandments presented by G-d in the Torah. '*Mitzvot*' in the plural.

Modeh Ani: The brief prayer recited immediately upon awakening, thanking G-d "for returning my soul to me."

Nachas: The quintessential Yiddish term referring to joy or pleasure, usually from one's children or grandchildren.

Narishkayt: Silliness, in Yiddish.

Oifruf: In Jewish tradition, a groom is called to read from the Torah, which takes place on the shabbat before his wedding.

Rosh yeshiva/rashei yeshivot: Dean, or "head of *yeshiva*," in Hebrew.

Rebbetzin: Wife of a rabbi. In this book, referring to Chaya Mushka Schneerson, wife of the Rebbe, who was also the middle daughter of the sixth Rebbe, Rabbi Yosef Yitzchak.

Shabbat: Torah's prescribed day of rest every Saturday.

Shema Yisrael: The fundamental utterance of Jewish faith. "Hear O Israel, the L-rd is our G-d, the L-rd is one."

Shidduch: A match for marriage.

Shliach/shlichus/shlucha: Emissary. In our case, referring to the young pairs of 'shliach' and 'shlucha,' male and female emissaries, whom the Rebbe would send to bring Torah and *mitzvot* to Jewish communities around the globe.

Siddur: Prayerbook.

'Sunday dollars:' Receiving line held by the Rebbe every Sunday at 770, in which he would hand each person a dollar to be given to the charity of their choice. Participants would use the brief meeting to ask for the Rebbe's advice or blessing.

Sukkot: Festival of Tabernacles.

Tachlis: Hebrew for purpose or bottom line.

Talmud: The key text of rabbinical Judaism, which contains the basis of Jewish law.

Tefillin: A pair of black leather boxes containing Hebrew parchment scrolls. A set includes two tefillin—one for the head and one for the arm. Tefillin are worn by Jewish men once a day, usually during morning prayers.

Tikkun: Spiritual rectification for a sin.

Tikkun olam: Hebrew for "to heal the world," referring to the Jewish responsibility "to perfect the world under the sovereignty of the Al-mighty."

Tzedaka: Hebrew for charity.

Tzedek: Justice.

Tzemach Tzedek: Third Rebbe of Chabad, Rabbi Menachem Mendel (1789–1866).

Tzitzit: Four cornered, fringed garment worn by Jewish males.

Yarmulke: Head covering for Jewish males.

Yechidut: Private audience with the Rebbe.

Yeshiva: Torah academy.

· MY ENCOUNTER WITH THE REBBE ·

Jewish Educational Media's *My Encounter with the Rebbe*
oral history project aims to document the life of the Rebbe,
Rabbi Menachem M. Schneerson, of righteous memory,
through first-person, videotaped, testimony.

The initiative attempts to study the Rebbe's life,
documenting the wisdom, sensitivity, and charisma
he displayed in his direct interactions with hundreds
of thousands of individuals, impacting their lives and,
ultimately, influencing the course of Judaism in his times.

To date, over 800 interviews have been conducted.
These recordings, along with the 20,000 pages of transcripts,
serve as an unparalleled primary resource for the historic
record, and as a source of inspiration for those who wish to
learn from and emulate the Rebbe's example.